The Cat & the Fiddle

Madeleine ~
Many thanks for
coming this evening
Jeremy Barlow

The Cat & the Fiddle

Images of musical humour from the Middle Ages to modern times

Jeremy Barlow

Bodleian Library
UNIVERSITY OF OXFORD

First published in 2006 by the Bodleian Library
Broad Street
Oxford OX1 3BG

www.bodleianbookshop.co.uk

ISBN: 1 85124 300 3
ISBN 13: 978 1 85124 300 6

Designed by Dot Little. Front cover design by Melanie Gradtke
Printed and bound by South Sea International Press, China
British Library Catalogue in Publishing Data
A CIP record of this publication is available from the British Library

For Ruth

———— ❧ ————

Contents

Preface

The images in *The Cat & the Fiddle* cover a period of some 750 years, and have been selected to highlight themes of graphic musical humour over the centuries. The progression of the book is more or less chronological, but I have from time to time interrupted the flow with a leap forward in time to show how artists have reused or reinvented illustrative devices. Not all the images will raise an immediate laugh; the humour may be hidden in a detail, or need explanation because of an unfamiliar historical context. Tastes change. Atrocious Victorian puns seem funny now, if at all, because they are so bad. Sometimes the humour forms part of a generally mocking tone, so amusement may depend on whether one enjoys the mockery or sympathizes with the mocked.

The principal sources and locations for humorous musical images shift over the centuries. This book focuses on the marginalia of English, Flemish, and French illuminated manuscripts up to the mid-fifteenth century, independent drawings and prints (particularly from the Low Countries in the sixteenth and seventeenth centuries), and then English drawings and prints in the eighteenth and nineteenth centuries. From the nineteenth century onwards, children's books, journals for adults, and sheet music covers provide material too. Illustrations have been selected chiefly from four remarkable collections that complement each other in covering these sources. Each collection was bequeathed to, or acquired by, the Bodleian Library, Oxford.

As I assembled my illustrations, one name more than any other kept cropping up in the Bodleian's catalogue references: 'Douce'. The name signifies an item originally belonging to Francis Douce (1757–1834), and it became apparent that his extensive interests included a penchant for grotesque, ludicrous, and satirical humour. Almost half the images in this book are from material that he bequeathed to the library, and include prints and drawings which were transferred from the Bodleian to the Ashmolean Museum in 1915.

Douce became a Fellow of the Society of Antiquaries in his early twenties (1779), and joined the Department of Manuscripts at the British Museum in 1807. He succeeded as Keeper shortly after, but grew unhappy in the post and left in 1811. It was said that 'he would neither bend nor bow to any man breathing'.[1] Late in life (1827) he received a considerable legacy from the estate of the sculptor Joseph Nollekens. He claimed that his new wealth had not brought him happiness, but it nevertheless enabled him to enlarge greatly his collection of manuscripts, books, drawings, prints, and coins. These he bequeathed to the Bodleian Library after a visit to Oxford in 1830. Francis Douce was a keen amateur pianist.

Other collections in the Bodleian that have provided material for this book are those of John Johnson, Iona and Peter Opie, and Walter Harding. John de Monins Johnson (1882–1956) held the post of Printer to the University at Oxford University Press from 1925 to 1946. As a hobby he collected ephemera and by the time of his death had amassed more than 1,000,000 items. He defined printed ephemera as 'everything which would ordinarily go into the waste paper basket after use, everything printed which is not actually a book ...'.[2] The images that I have chosen from his collection could hardly be defined as waste-paper-basket material. Johnson's collection

was transferred from Oxford University Press to the
Bodleian in 1968.

Iona Opie (b. 1923) and her husband Peter Opie
(1918–82) made their joint reputation with the *Oxford
Dictionary of Nursery Rhymes* (1951). During their
research they began to collect children's books, and
by the time of Peter Opie's death they had gathered
some 20,000 titles. Iona Opie decided to sell the
collection to the Bodleian, if money could be raised.
Prince Charles led a national appeal which raised
£500,000, half the value of the collection. Iona Opie
donated the other half.

Walter N. H. Harding, though London born,
emigrated to Chicago with his parents at the age of
four and spent the rest of his life there. He was a
versatile keyboard player; on piano for silent movies
and music hall, and as organist at several Chicago
churches and his Masonic lodge. His wide-ranging
music collection was transferred to the Bodleian
during 1975 (in 900 packing cases), and it includes
about 100,000 American songs from *c.* 1800 onwards.

It is said that Francis Douce left his collections
to the Bodleian because he was treated with such
courtesy on his visit to the library in 1830, even
though the librarian did not know who he was or
what he possessed. I too have received great kindness
and assistance from the staff at the library. First
I must thank Rigmor Båtsvik, Picture Librarian.
I came to her in the first instance for slides to
illustrate a lecture on the imagery of musical humour.
Almost at once she suggested a book on the subject
and I am very grateful to Samuel Fanous, Head of
Communications & Publishing, for taking on the
project so readily, and to Emily Jolliffe for seeing it
through the editorial process. Other members of staff
who have been particularly helpful include Michael

Heaney, Oxford University Library Services, Clive Hurst, Head of Rare Books, Julie Anne Lambert, Librarian of the John Johnson Collection, and Peter Ward Jones, Music Librarian. I must also thank Kate Heard and Caroline Newman at the Print Room of the Ashmolean Museum.

1   Quoted in *The Douce Legacy: An exhibition to commemorate the 150th anniversary of the bequest of Francis Douce (1757–1834)* (Oxford, Bodleian Library, 1984), p. ix, from Thomas Frognall Dibdin's *Reminiscences of a Literary Life* (1836).
2   *The John Johnson Collection: Catalogue of an Exhibition* (Oxford, 1971), 11.

I

Marginal Musicians

TITANIA What, wilt thou hear some music, my sweet love?
BOTTOM (with ass's head) I have a reasonable good ear in music. Let us have the tongs and the bones.
Music tongs, rural music.

In this exchange between spellbound lovers from *A Midsummer Night's Dream*,[1] Shakespeare combines two enduring devices of musical humour over the centuries: animals substituting for humans, and the use of implements as mock instruments.

Both devices occur in illuminations for psalters dating from the thirteenth and fourteenth centuries. Such psalters might have belonged to a monastery, but rich families also commissioned them, as a kind of status symbol. Medieval illuminators showed scant respect for the sacred context of their art as they embellished the margins and initials. Lewdness abounds, both scatological and sexual, and the general antics of humans, hybrids, animals, and monsters often bear no discernible relation to the accompanying psalm or collect. Sometimes a modicum of decorum is observed. In a Psalter made for St Augustine's Abbey, Canterbury, during the first quarter of the thirteenth century, a fox blowing

1. **Fox blows horn**.
c. 1200–25. Illumination in initial C(onfessioni nostre piam aurem), for the Collect at the end of Psalm 10. Psalter for St Augustine's Abbey, Canterbury. Creatures of many species decorate the initials to the collects in this Psalter; the fox is the most popular animal. Foxes and hares blow the horn that is used to hunt them in a number of medieval illuminations and church sculptures. Here, the instrument could also be interpreted as a small shawm, the raucous double-reed ancestor of the oboe.

2. **Fiddler, imitated by ape with stick**. *c.* 1320–30. Illumination at the end of Psalm 109:19. Portable Psalter, Ghent. The instrument being aped is a medieval fiddle; the tuning pegs indicate three strings, and there are suggestions of frets on the fingerboard.

3. **Mock fiddler with bellows and tongs**. *c.* 1300. Illumination at the start of the collect following Psalm 16, Ormesby Psalter, East Anglia. Is the figure a hybrid, with a red, lizard-like lower half, or is the lizard a separate creature (the small feet face backwards) snuffling up under the player's apron or skirt? The tip of the bellows points at a similar blue creature coiled within the initial C(onserva nos Domine) for the start of the collect. This Psalter contains various strange beasts and hybrids; their spotted backs are a feature in other illuminated manuscripts too.

a horn or shawm (**1**) forms one of many humorous animal designs found in initials to the collects (prayers) that follow each psalm. Initials to the psalms themselves, on the other hand, are historiated with religious scenes.

An animal frequently encountered in margins is the monkey or ape, usually behaving mischievously. In an early fourteenth-century Flemish Psalter the ape apes the fiddler above him with a stick as a mock bow (**2**), and one wonders what possible relationship there might be to the adjoining text from Psalm 109:19: 'Fiat et sicut vestimentum quo operitur et sicut zona qua semper praecingitur' (May it be like a garment which covereth him; and like a girdle with which he is girded continually). Some medieval writers used the word 'babewyn' (Chaucer's spelling for 'baboon')[2] to describe grotesque creatures generally, whether human, monstrous, hybrid, or animal. Another term was 'monster'. I shall use the word 'grotesque' as a general term, although it originated later (it derives from descriptions of the fantastical decorations in a palace of the Emperor Nero, unearthed in grottos near Rome in the late fifteenth century).

Over many centuries the most popular implements used as mock musical instruments have been domestic and kitchen equipment, especially fire irons: tongs, bellows, the gridiron, and so on. The use of bellows and tongs to depict a mock fiddler in the margins of the Ormesby Psalter **(3)** is echoed more than 600 years later in a tableau of bellows-and-tongs sketches by the nineteenth century caricaturist George Cruikshank **(4)**. Today we perceive such implements simply as incongruous pictorial substitutes for proper musical instruments, but from the Middle Ages to the nineteenth century they may have had additional significance from their use in noisy demonstrations of celebration or protest known by the French term *charivari* (an old English expression was 'rough music'). A *charivari* could be occasioned by a wedding celebration on the one hand (the tying of tin cans and other objects to the newly-wed couple's car is a remnant of the ritual) and as an expression of disapproval at marital cruelty or infidelity on the other.

The juxtaposition of the profane and sacred in medieval art puzzles modern commentators, and a much-quoted passage[3] from an address written by the Cistercian abbot St Bernard in the first part of the twelfth century shows that it puzzled the medieval critic too. St Bernard was commenting on the use of

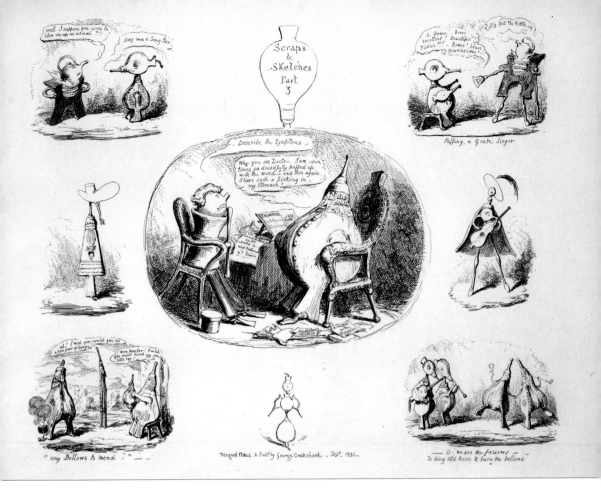

4. **Scraps and Sketches Part 3**. 1831. Print, George Cruikshank (1792–1878). The illustrations above combine visual and verbal musical punning through the use of bellows and other objects. Top right, for example, we have a man formed from a fire grate and kettle. He sings 'Polly put the Kettle on', while the seated listener, constructed from bellows, applauds 'O Bravo! Bravo! Excellent! Beautiful! Divine!!! – Bravo! bravo! Bravissimo!!!' The caption under reads 'Puffing a Grate Singer'.

grotesques in church carvings, but his remarks could apply equally to illuminated manuscripts:

What are those lascivious apes doing, those fierce lions, monstrous centaurs, half-men and spotted leopards … ? You can see several bodies attached to one head, or, the other way round, many heads joined to one body. Here a serpent's tail is to be seen on a four-footed beast, there a fish with an animal's head. There is a creature starting out as a horse, whilst the back end of a goat brings up the rear; here a horned beast generates the rear of a horse. Indeed there are so many things, and everywhere such an extraordinary variety of hybrid forms, that it is more diverting … to spend the whole day gazing on such singularities in preference to meditating on God's laws.

A hybrid of the kind described by St Bernard is to be found playing a rebec or fiddle in a mid-fifteenth century French Book of Hours (5). During the previous century the Book of Hours had supplanted the Psalter as the favoured devotional compendium of the rich. Books of Hours included prayers that were to be recited at particular times of day, as well as further prayers, psalms, and a liturgical calendar (it was customary in the Middle Ages to read any text out loud, whether sacred or secular).

Other marginal creatures found in Psalters and Books of Hours include demons or devils, as for example the red-faced horned fellow with hand-bells approaching an angel trumpeter in another early fourteenth-century Flemish Psalter (6). Devils featured in medieval mystery plays, and a sense of dramatic performance often comes across in the antics of marginal grotesques (is the demon dancing?). As Shakespeare reminds us in *A Midsummer Night's Dream*, the uses of humour in performance may be closely linked to representations in graphic imagery.

5. **Hybrid fiddler**. *c*.1450–70. From the circle of Maître François and assistants. Illumination, Book of Hours (fragment), France. The hybrid has a human upper half (his hood has ears, suggesting a fool's cap; see p. 24), with hoofed legs and a tail. The instrument has three strings and, unusually, two circular sound-holes.

2
Animal Amusements

So far, the medieval images selected have come from sacred works. An important genre of illuminated manuscript with secular subject matter was the romance, in which the fabulous adventures and feats of a historic figure such as Charlemagne, King Arthur, or Alexander the Great were narrated. One of the finest manuscripts in the Bodleian Library is *Li romans du boin roi Alixandre* (referred to as *The Romance of Alexander*), a fifteenth-century Flemish version of the tale, written in Picard French. Sumptuous full-page illustrations relate to the story, but only occasionally can one discern a relationship between marginal drolleries and text.

Illustrations in *The Romance of Alexander* include a huge number of musicians (about 250). Some play from ramparts or indoors in the full-page pictures; others adorn the margins, along with birds, beasts, and decorative foliage. Along the bottom of the pages (the *bas de page*) musicians often accompany sports, games, entertainments, and unexplained rituals. Musical humour may form a detail, unnoticed at first. In the image of a gittern player accompanying dancers (**7**), it is the animal heads of the latter that first catch the attention. But look closely at the gittern. Decorating the end of the peg box is a head (a feature found on many surviving viols and citterns

6. **Demon plays hand bells at angel trumpeter**. *c.*1320–30. Illumination, Psalter, Ghent. The demon seems to be taunting the angel trumpeter with his bell-ringing. The trumpeter gestures at him with his forefinger. Note the strange creature standing on the left and looking away.

7. Gittern player accompanies dancers. 1338–44. Workshop of Jehan de Grise. *Bas de page* illumination from *The Romance of Alexander*. The musician accompanies the dancers with a gittern, an ancestor of the guitar. The three male dancers wear animal heads: stag, hare, and boar. They link hands with two women and seem to be dancing.

8. Musicians frame dice players. 1338–44. Workshop of Jehan de Grise. *Bas de page* illumination from *The Romance of Alexander*. Those involved in the game of dice are framed by three performers on plucked instruments: a psaltery player on the left, a gittern player on the right, and a harpist above, in a decorated initial.

from the Renaissance period), and the head seems to be grinning at the player. The animal-headed dancers grimace towards the player too. In another scene, a gittern player performs while an intently focused group watches a game of dice **(8)**; here the instrument's head peers down at the dicers. Above on the left is a large initial, embellished with a harpist. The harp has a head too, which stares back at the player.

Although marginal activities often convey a sense of performance, our knowledge of occasions for music in the Middle Ages is incomplete, so it may not be possible to judge the extent to which an illustrator is being realistic or tongue-in-cheek. Animated gittern heads are an impossibility, but did dancers with animal heads exist, and did they

9. **The Beggar's Opera burlesqued**. 1728. Print. John Gay (1685–1732) conceived *The Beggar's Opera* as an English antithesis to the Italian operas which had dominated London's musical scene in the 1710s and 1720s. Here the leading protagonists are given animal heads: the gaoler Lockit (ox), his daughter Lucy (pig), the highwayman hero Macheath (ass), Polly Peachum (cat), her father Peachum (fox), and her mother Mrs Peachum (bird). An Italian opera performance has been pushed into the background. Instruments in the burlesque band comprise a bagpipe, saltbox (see **18** and **32**), jew's harp, dulcimer, and bladder-and-string (see **32** and **36**).

perform to music in the manner shown? The tradition of performance with animal masks goes back to classical antiquity, and was certainly present in the Middle Ages. In the early fifteenth century the Bishop of Nantes forbade popular entertainers from using 'monstra larvarum'[4] (grotesque masks). Four hundred years after *The Romance of Alexander*, a satire on the popularity of *The Beggar's Opera* during its first London run in 1728 displays similar animal heads **(9)** (see also the mock instruments in the accompanying band). Before the industrial revolution in the nineteenth century, most people lived in a rural environment, and at all levels of society had closer involvement with the animals that they hunted, trained for hunting, and ate.

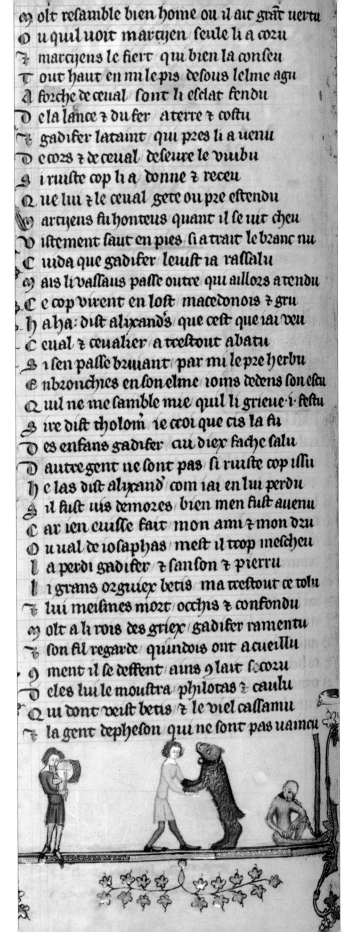

10. **Pipe and taborer accompanies dancing bear**. 1338–44. Workshop of Jehan de Grise. *Bas de page* illumination from *The Romance of Alexander*. A youth playing pipe and tabor accompanies a similar figure dancing with a bear. On the far right an ape chained to a post examines itself lewdly.

don't be afraid of my Bear Ladies & Gentlemen, I have tamed & muzzeled him & reform'd his Habits

The BEAR and his LEADER "what tho I am Obligated to Dance a Bear, a Man may be a Gentleman for all that, My Bear ever dances to the Gentelest of Tunes

Animals were trained for entertainment too. The bear, dancing to music, could be seen from the Middle Ages until the nineteenth century, and illustrators transformed the familiar image for humorous purposes. The bear might be given a human, quizzical expression, as it dances with a human **(10)**, a recognizable face **(11)**, or have its talents transferred to a less plausible beast: a sow, suckling her piglets, for example **(12)**. The latter jest recurs many centuries later, as a bagpiper sow plays to her dancing piglets on the cover to a Victorian children's tale **(13)**.

Occasionally, an illustrator directed humour at the learned musician rather than the popular entertainer. A volume containing the Statutes of England (*c.* 1500), shows an owl as a musical director or instructor, holding open a score **(14)**. An ape supports the score; his open mouth suggests that he is singing. He stares, a little anxiously perhaps, at the owl. From the same period comes a Flemish drawing of an ass playing the

11. ***The Bear and his Leader.*** From *Caricatures of Gillray. c.* 1818 (print originally published 1806). James Gillray (1757–1815). Gillray produced many political satires directed at Charles James Fox (1749–1806), an MP with radical sympathies. Here Fox is the muzzled and chained bear. The other three politicians represented are Lord Sidmouth (formerly Henry Addington) as a blind fiddler with bogus wooden leg (see **26**) playing 'God save the King', Lord Henry Petty as a diminutive monkey holding a fool's cap with coxcomb and bell (see **20**), and Lord Grenville as the bear's owner. George III had recently appointed Grenville as Prime Minister, and the latter had made Fox his Foreign Secretary (Fox resented a subordinate role). Addington was a former Prime Minister.

23

12. Performing sow with suckling piglets. 1338–44. Workshop of Jehan de Grise. *Bas de page* illumination from *The Romance of Alexander*. A drummer accompanies a performing sow with piglets. On the left an owl looks puzzled (decorations for the page include many other birds).

13. Cover illustration for *The Tragic & Yet Strictly Moral Story of How Three Little Pigs Went to Market and the Old One Stayed at Home*. *c.*1878. Charles Altamont Doyle (1832–93). The story, set to music, tells how mother pig sends three little pigs to market to buy ingredients for a pancake. They quarrel on the way home, and after hurling the flour, milk, sugar, and eggs at each other, fall in a muddy ditch:

> And they looked so much like batter,
> Only richer far and fatter.
> The old pig, mad as a hatter,
> Put them all in the frying-pan.

The old pig fries and eats the little pigs, and dies of indigestion. The title page includes some excruciating puns (see also **4** and **41**), with the claim that the story is related in 'EGGS-HAMETER, ILLUSTRATED WITH CUTS FROM BACON, AND PRINTED IN PIGMENT.'

organ **(15)**. An open score is again visible; it signified musical learning at a time when oral transmission played a much greater part in music-making than it does today. The ass makes an appropriate animal to burlesque serious musicianship, on account of his unmusical bray and large ears (Bottom's 'good ear in music'). At the Feast of Fools, held by clerics just after Christmas, sacrilegious behaviour included braying as a substitute for responses in the mass. Stylized ass's ears had been a feature of the Fool's outfit since Roman times.

14. **Owl and ape with musical score**. *c.*1500. Marginal illumination, the Statutes of England to 1495. The image heads a page of statutes that includes the Magna Carta.

15. **Ass plays organ**. *c.*1480. Pen and bistre, School of Hugo van der Goes. An ass, fastened into a barrel-shaped chair, plays a positive organ. Behind the organ a woman operates the bellows. A man feeds a thistle to the ass.

16. **Dog hybrid plays rebec**. *c.*1450–60. Marginal illumination, Book of Hours, Bayeux, use of Bayeux. The rebec came to be associated with the itinerant musician and entertainer. By the mid-fifteenth century it had three strings, tuned in fifths as on a modern violin.

During the fourteenth and fifteenth centuries, the margins of illuminated manuscripts became filled with increasingly rich floral decoration; the development of this process may be seen by comparing the *Romance of Alexander* borders with the detail from the Statutes of England manuscript 150 years later. Eventually, grotesque musicians have no place in such prettiness, though in a mid-fifteenth century French Book of Hours an insouciant rebec-playing dog hybrid steps forth amid richly coloured foliage **(16)**; see also the hybrid fiddler in **(5)**.

No 69 A° 1539 Jar liessen drey Haubtman

3

Carnival, Coxcombs, and Commedia

The change in style of marginal decoration and the simultaneous development of the printed book shifted the principal location for musical humour in the Renaissance to the independent drawing, print, or painting. The subject matter and illustrations of early printed books (incunabula) sometimes influenced representations in art, and in entertainment too. One of the most successful books from the late fifteenth century was Sebastian Brant's *Narrenschiff* (Ship of Fools). Brant satirized man's follies through the traditional figure of the Fool. Follies are categorized, and various types of fool are then shipped off to the Land of Fools. An illustrated manuscript record of Shrovetide (*Fastnacht*) Carnivals in Nuremberg between 1449 and 1539 shows a Ship of Fools as a float in the celebrations of 1539 **(17)** (the picture is a later copy). On board are two fools, alongside academics, musicians, and beasts. Subversive humour, expressed through grotesque costumes, masks, ribald behaviour, music, dance, and elements of *charivari* have remained essential ingredients of Carnival celebrations to this day. A group of figures symbolizing Carnival **(18)**, adapted from a detail of Bruegel's *Battle between Carnival and Lent*, includes mock instruments: a woman plays a saltbox and a masked man strums on a gridiron.

17. **A Ship of Fools**. 1640 (copied from an earlier record of 1539). Schembartbuch. Watercolour, probably by Hanns Ammon, Nuremberg. The two fools wear traditional multicoloured costumes and hoods with stylized ass's ears and bells. The figures close to the mast have been identified as academics. One holds a backgammon board (the devil's game), while the other stares at a flask containing a yellow liquid. In the prow sits a steersman, while a trumpeter heralds the float's progress through Nuremberg. In the lookout are two further musicians: a bombard (large shawm) player and a bagpiper. A horned beast holds what appears to be a key, and another indistinct object. A further academic examines a globe.

18. **Composition of seven figures symbolizing Carnival**. Date unknown. Pen and wash, after Pieter Bruegel the elder. This drawing is based on a detail from Bruegel's *Battle of Carnival and Lent* (1559). It shows the jolly, rotund figures representing Carnival, who, in Bruegel's painting, confront the miserable, emaciated figures of Lent. The artist has changed several of Bruegel's figures, and commentators believe the drawing to be of a much later date.

The Italian form of masked theatre that became known as the *commedia dell'arte* is often associated with Carnival in surviving records of its early history. *Commedia* troupes travelled widely, and influenced theatre in France, England, and other countries during the seventeenth and eighteenth centuries. As part of the semi-improvised and gestural style of acting, *commedia* performers might turn a stage prop into an imaginary object: sit facing backwards astride a chair and it becomes a horse. In the mock instrument tradition, a French *Polichinelle* (*Pulcinella* in Italian, and the ancestor of Punch in England) holds a gridiron and tongs as fiddle and bow **(19)**. The resemblance of the name *Pulcinella* to the Italian *pulcino* for 'chick' or 'chicken' has suggested to theatre historians that his origins may be linked

Polichinelle.
Si Polichinelle à grand mine   Son Cœur Scait brauer le peril
Arme de Pincette, et de Gril: Que l'on rencontre à la Cuisine.

19. **Polichinelle**. Mid-seventeenth century. Print. Images of the Italian *commedia* character *Pulcinella* begin to appear in the seventeenth century, and show his characteristic humpback, hooked nose, and tall hat. The association of a humpback with a hooked nose mask survive in images of stock types from Greek and Roman comic theatre. *Pulcinella*, like his English descendant Punch, characteristically displayed a mixture of stupidity, wit, cunning, and villainy.

20. **A feast with mummers**. Late sixteenth century. Pen and wash, Flemish, attributed to Jan Verbeeck. The grotesque musician here is the small figure dressed as a cockerel and playing the pipe and tabor, to the left of the man with a club. To the right of the latter, cockerels' heads are being dispensed to a couple with plates. Diners eat the unappetizing fare at the long table above. On the balcony to the left a choir sings from a large book.

to the tradition of the Fool. The Fool's hood, as well as sporting ass's ears, often had a ridge or peak from front to back: a stylized cock's comb (Shakespeare used the expression 'coxcomb' abusively, meaning fool).

An odd, repellent use of cockerel imagery comes in a sixteenth-century Flemish drawing of a feast with mummers **(20)**. The intricate detail of the scene suggests at first that the artist has taken pains to depict an actual occasion. Several medieval and Renaissance pictures record mummers in exotic costumes entering great halls to perform; here the mummers are wearing bird outfits. But doubts about the realism of the scene arise as one discovers that diners at the banquet are being served with cockerels' heads. The centrally placed verses are enigmatic in translation, and begin 'We do not know how to speak, but we do not want to remain silent'.

Commedia imagery finds its way into an Italian satire on artistic patronage, probably dating from the seventeenth century (**21**). The patron of the arts seldom attracts satirical attention during the Renaissance and early Baroque periods; professional artists do not bite the hand that feeds them. Yet here is a patron who sits, bloated and passive in the *commedia* ruff associated with the character *Pierrot*, amidst evidence of artistic labours on his behalf. An elderly painter works away, and a *Pulcinella*-like figure sings from a score supported by a figure in a peaked hat while an impoverished musician directs over his shoulder. A cupid holds aloft a washing line with freshly composed scores hung out to dry.

21. **A patron of the arts**. Date unknown. Pen and watercolours, attributed to Faustino Bocchi (1659–1742). The score being sung on the right has partly obscured words: CANT at the top and DI LVCA MARE at the bottom. The latter words probably refer to the composer Luca Marenzio (c.1553–99), who was born near Brescia and studied there; the artist Faustino Bocchi worked in the city more than a century later. The *Pulcinella*-like figure could be singing the *canto* (highest) part from one of Marenzio's 500 madrigals. There are puzzling features to this drawing in relation to the attribution. Although Marenzio was renowned in the late sixteenth century, his works would have seemed old-fashioned by Bocchi's time. Yet the music hanging to dry seems to suggest that the patron demands freshly composed material.

22. **The Rich Kitchen**. 1563.
Print, Jerome Cock, from a
drawing by Pieter Bruegel the
elder (*c*.1525–69). Bruegel
supplied some 130 drawings
to Jerome Cock's renowned
Antwerp engraving workshop,
as the subjects for prints.
Bruegel's name as the designer
appears in the top right hand
corner, and Cock's diagonally
opposite, lower left. In the
companion print, *The Poor
Kitchen*, thin, stick-like men
make the best of a dish of
oysters, while a fat man tries to
escape from a similarly placed
door.

4
Social Satire

Although the word 'satire' is used loosely for any kind
of biting humour, dictionaries define it as ridicule
or irony used to expose false pretensions, vice, and
folly (as in Brant's *Narrenschiff*). Some genre drawings,
prints, and paintings of the sixteenth and seventeenth
centuries depict low-life and rustic scenes without
any apparent moral message, while others have a
distinctly satirical tone. Musicians at the lower end
of the professional scale often find themselves drawn
into the satire and humour of genre scenes. Bruegel
employed his favourite instrumentalist, the bagpiper,
in a two-part satire on gluttony, *The Rich Kitchen* **(22)**
and *The Poor Kitchen* (not shown). In the former print,
the emaciated player is being ejected from a scene of
obese and rotund figures. Poverty is to be ignored in a
world of greed. In a wedding scene **(23)** (after Adriaen
van de Venne), the stolid bagpiper inspires frenetic
dancing, yet sits impassively between a man vomiting
and a dog licking a baby's bottom.

Another low-status instrumentalist associated
with rustic humour during the seventeenth and
eighteenth centuries is the hurdy-gurdy player. The
instrument sounds similar to the bagpipe because
the wheel that rubs against the strings produces a
sound uninterrupted by breath or change of bow, and
because it too makes use of a drone (an unchanging

23. **A rustic marriage feast**. Date unknown. Black lead drawing, after Adriaen van de Venne (1589–1662). The bride is seated in the background, at a table, just right of centre. Much more prominence is given to the vigorous dance, foreground left, and to the activities either side of the bagpiper. The Dutch artist Adriaen van de Venne was a poet as well as an artist; he worked in Middleburg and The Hague.

24. ***L'espousée de vilage***.
Seventeenth century. Print.
Although the picture seems
mocking in tone, verses
underneath state that the
bridegroom and pregnant bride
deserve praise rather than
mockery, for they proclaim
openly that love is good, and
consent innocently to the laws
of wedlock.

LESPOVSEE DE VILAGE.

Cet Espous et cette Espousée
Parmy leurs amoureux deuis,
Sont plus dignes à mon aduis
De louange que de risée

Ils disent sans deguisement
Qu'aimer est vne belle chose;
Et flechissent innocemment
Soubs les loix qu'Hymen leur jmpose.

Mariette excud.

note that accompanies the tune). Artists used both instruments to signify the bucolic life. In *L'espousée de vilage* (The village bride) **(24)** a hurdy-gurdy player leers knowingly at us, next to the pregnant bride. French hurdy-gurdy players, particularly from the Savoie region, came to England in large numbers to find work during the eighteenth century. A political satire about 100 years later **(25)** exploited the Duke of Cumberland's rumoured affair with a young Savoyard player. Gossipers relished the contrasts of class, age, and nationality between the duke and his mistress.

25. *John of Gant in Love*. 1749. Print. 'John of Gant' refers to William Augustus, the Duke of Cumberland (1721–65), who ruthlessly defeated the 1745 Jacobite Rebellion. The nickname derives from the duke's more recent failure to capture the city of Ghent (the original John of Gaunt's birthplace). The print is anonymous, probably to avoid censorship or reprisal.

John of Gant in Love, or Mars on his knees.
Musick hath Charms to sooth the Savage Breast!
To Soften Rocks, and bend the Knotted Oak.
Congrave.
Price 6.ᵈ
Published According to Act of Parliament July 15.ᵗʰ

26. **Armoe soeckt List**. Date unknown. Print, after Adriaen van de Venne (1589–1662). The title translates as 'Poverty leads to cunning'. It alludes to the fiddler's pretended blindness and to his bogus wooden leg. His real leg is shown bent round, with his wrapped foot hidden behind (see also **11**). In the background stands a man playing a jew's harp, another instrument played by street itinerants (see **9**).

27. **Cochalino Inamorato qual, Sfogg l'Ardor sua col Canto uerso la sua Diva**. 1642. From *Il Carnevale Italiano Mascherato* (The Italian Masked Carnival), a set of 23 prints by F. Bertelli. The title translates 'Cochalino in love displays ardour with his song about his goddess'. The instrument is an archlute or theorbo, which has long bass strings stretching out to a second peg box.

28. **From Merry England**. 1956. Ronald Searle (b.1920). Ronald Searle has enjoyed satirizing the habits and manners of the twentieth-century bourgeoisie, and here he makes fun of the staid ballroom dancing scene in the 1950s, just before the rock'n'roll revolution.

During the seventeenth century, the impoverished, blind, one-legged fiddler **(26)** joins the bagpiper and hurdy-gurdy player as a stereotyped itinerant musician (see also **11** and **34**). Poverty, disability, and old age were all considered fair game for mockery and satire at the time. Among a set of Italian *commedia* prints from 1642, a serenading lutenist (called *Cochalino*) has been given *Pulcinella*'s humpback and the mask of an elderly man with a beaky nose **(27)** (*Cochalino* and *Pulcino* have a similar meaning). The comical aspiration of the serenader, so near yet so far from his beloved, has been a recurrent topic in theatrical and graphic humour. In amorous scenes generally, musicians are forever condemned to making music, not love; they cannot do both simultaneously. However, 300 years after *Cochalino*, Ronald Searle attempted to resolve the dilemma by

Armoe soeckt List.

portraying a gigolo who plays the guitar behind his
dance partner's back **(28)**.

The use of masks and animal musicians continues
in a seventeenth-century Flemish drawing of *The
Temptation of St Anthony*, in the manner of David
Teniers **(29)**. The torments suffered by the long-
lived St Anthony of Egypt (251–356 CE) were a
popular subject with artists over several centuries,
and constitute one of the few religious subjects
to incorporate grotesque imagery. Sometimes the

saint is depicted as being confronted with beautiful women, naked or clothed, but more often he is beset with unenticing monsters. Here, a décolleté young woman stands near the saint, but she is outnumbered by an array of beasts and hybrids; some of the latter could be humans with animal masks.

The grotesque animal imagery of Teniers and others from the Low Countries found its way to England, as the seventeenth-century artist Francis Barlow demonstrates in an obscure political satire **(30)**.

29. **The Temptation of St Anthony**. Seventeenth century. Pen and wash, imitator of David Teniers (1610–90). Musicians appear among the grotesques, and include creatures on trumpet, tambourine, triangle, fiddle, and shawm. Between the tambourine player and fiddler stands a singer.

41

30. **A political satire**. 1679. Pen and wash, Francis Barlow (?1626–1702). According to one interpretation, the jousting match symbolizes a struggle over the dukedom of Lorraine, which Louis XIV (the ape riding the boar) had taken from the Holy Roman Emperor, Leopold I (the ape on the bear) and then ceded back to the duke. The owl blowing a horn represents the papacy, and the snipe may represent Charles XI of Sweden, then an ally of Louis XIV. The squires, shown as monkeys walking behind the animals, are the Duke of Lorraine on the left and Charles II of England on the right (Charles had signed the Dover treaty with Louis XIV in 1670) (D. B. Brown, *Ashmolean Museum Oxford: Catalogue of the Collection of Drawings*, iv: *The Earlier British Drawings* (Oxford, 1982), 41).

Diarist John Evelyn called Barlow the 'famous painter of Fowle, Beasts and Birds',[5] and here an owl and a snipe oppose each other with differently-shaped horns. A more obvious political message lies behind the use of musical mockery in Charles I's penultimate court masque before the outbreak of civil war. Near the opening of *Britannia Triumphans*, the playwright Sir William Davenant included a series of six antimasque dances performed by low-class characters in a 'horrid hell' **(31)** (the antimasque preceded the masque proper, and consisted of humorous, exotic, or grotesque material). First to enter is a *charivari* of street musicians playing *mockmusick* on instruments that include the now familiar tongs and gridiron. Among other performers in the dances that follow are *commedia* characters (the Doctor, a Zany, and Harlequin), two baboons and an ape, parasitical courtiers, and past rebellious leaders in war. The inclusion of the latter group and our knowledge of Charles's struggle with Parliamentarians makes the meaning clear: unruly forces threaten the monarch's authority, and vindicate his determination to rule without Parliament. All the devices of mockery we have encountered so far have been incorporated into the scene: low-class musicians, mock instruments, and animals.

10 *Britannia Triumphans.*

The whole Scene was transformed into a horrid Hell,
the further part terminating in a flaming precipice,
and the neerer parts expressing the Suburbs, from
whence enter the severall Antimasques.

1. Entrie.
Of mockmusick of 5. persons.
One with a Violl, the rest with
Taber and Pipe,
Knackers and bells,
Tongs and key,
Gridiron and shooing horne.

2. Entrie.
A ballad singer
his companion } *with their Auditorie.*
A Porter laden,
A Vineners boy,
A Saylor.

3. Entrie.
A crier of mouse-traps,
A seller of tinderboxes, } *bearing the Engines be-*
longing to their trades.
The master of
Two Baboones and
An Ape.

4. Entrie.
A Mountebanke in the habit of a grave Doctor,
A Zany
A Harlekin } *his men.*
An old lame Charewoman.
Two Pale menches presenting their urinals, and hee
distributing his printed receits out of a Budget.

5. Entrie.

Britannia Triumphans. 11

5. Entrie.
Foure old fashioned Parasiticall Courtiers.

6. Entrie.
Of rebellious Leaders in warre.
Cade,
Kett,
Jack Straw *and*
their souldiers.

The apparell of these in part shewed their base professions, mixt with some souldier-like Accoutre-
ments.

These Antimasques being past, *Bellerophon* entered
riding on *Pegasus*, in a cote armour of silver scales, and
on his head an Antique Helme with Plumes, his Bases

The *Pegasus* was covered all with white close to his
hand, the point of lead.

The *Pegasus* was covered all with white close to his
skin, his main and tail of silver, with large white
wings, his reines and saddle of carnation trim'd with
silver. Hee riding up into the middle of the roome
with an attendant alighted.

Action.

Bellerophon? *Thou that the of-spring art of Heaven,*
Most timely, and by Inspiration sure,
Thou com'st to helpe me to despise and scorne
These Ayry mimick Apparitions, which
This cosening Prophet would present as great
Examples for succeeding times to imitate.

B 3   Belle-

---

31. **Antimasque scene in**
Britannia Triumphans.
1638. Inigo Jones and William
Davenant. The two pages
describe a series of six danced
'entries' (each equivalent to
an 'entrée' in French ballet)
of disreputable characters.
Sketches by Inigo Jones of the
performers survive in the Duke
of Devonshire's collection; the
anomalous viol player in the
mockmusick entry (the viol
being an instrument associated
then with respectable amateurs
of the gentry and nobility) turns
out to be a street fiddler.

5
Class Contrasts

32. **Frontispiece for *The Jovial Companions or Merry Club***. 1709. Print, Henry Hulsbergh (*fl.* 1703–24, *d.* 1729), after a design by Marcellus Laroon the younger (1679–1772). The artist, musician, and soldier Marcellus Laroon the younger assembled a fearsome ensemble of street musicians: a singer with tongs and key, a shawm player, a ballad singer with clown's ruff, a fiddler, another ballad singer, a player on bladder-and-string, and a singer with saltbox.

There are no political inferences to be drawn from the group of street performers and mock instruments **(32)** assembled at the start of the eighteenth century as the frontispiece to a book of catches called *The Jovial Companions or Merry Club*. Here, the idea was to burlesque the gentlemen who met together in convivial clubs to sing 'celebrated catches compos'd by the late Mr Henry Purcell & Dr Blow'.[6] Why make fun of such an apparently commendable activity? The answer may be that, despite the eminence of the composers, the lyrics of the catches are often bawdy in the extreme.

William Hogarth, the greatest graphic satirist of the eighteenth century, incorporated musical

details into many of his works. In a print from the 12-part series *Industry & Idleness* **(33)** he included two competing groups of performers that traditionally turned up at weddings to mark the celebrations with a noisy *charivari*: drummers and butchers' boys on marrowbones and specially tuned cleavers. In his preliminary sketches, Hogarth showed only the drummers. The butchers' boys, plus the unfortunate cellist and the ballad singer, add conflict and humour to the final print. Forty years later, *May-Day in London* (engraved by William Blake after Samuel Collings's design) **(34)** brings together various performers who took part in the traditional festivities; included is another *charivari*, performed by chimney sweeps with brushes and shovels. Jumping forward a further 70 years, the theme of street hubbub is continued by the *Punch* artist John Leech, in a print called, ironically, *The Quiet Street* **(35)**. There were many complaints against street musicians from Victorian citizenry, and Leech has assembled, from left to right, a German band, an Italian mechanical organ (objections were tinged with xenophobia), and various singers performing hits of the day. Such scenes provide information for the social historian, but should not be taken as literal, snapshot representations of particular occasions.

Switching back to the mid-eighteenth century, we move up the social scale in *The Consort* **(36)**. The anonymous artist has drawn grotesque figures with oversized heads (known as Callot figures, after the caricature style of the seventeenth-century French printmaker Jacques Callot). The placing of such an orchestra and audience in open parkland is an unlikely scenario, but may allude to the concerts at fashionable pleasure gardens in London such as Vauxhall, Ranelagh, and Marylebone (where players

Married to his Master's Daughter.

Publish'd according to Act of Parliament Sep.tr 30.1747

33. *Industry & Idleness 6: The Industrious 'Prentice out of his Time and Married to his Master's Daughter*. 1747. Print, William Hogarth (1697–1764). William Hogarth's twelve-part moral tale *Industry & Idleness* contrasts the fortunes of two apprentices, one hard-working and the other lazy and dishonest. Here, halfway through the series, the industrious apprentice has completed his apprenticeship and married his master's daughter. At the wedding celebrations the bride is paying off the drummers. The disabled ballad singer promotes a song ('Jesse or the Happy Pair' by William Boyce) that extols the joys of married life.

Collings del.   *Blake sculp.*

MAY-DAY IN LONDON.

34. *May-Day in London.*
1784. Print, William Blake (1757–1827), after a design by Samuel Collings (*fl.* 1780–91). Several descriptions and illustrations survive of traditional May Day celebrations in London. Milkmaids danced to a fiddler, and their milk pails, carried on the head, were adorned with tankards and other ware, known as 'garlands'. Imitating or parodying them were bunters (rag-collectors), with an inverted basket similarly adorned. Here, the milkmaid is on the left, her body hidden behind a man quaffing, and the bunter, visible, is on the right. Boy chimney sweeps also took part; they dressed in smart clothes and played mock instruments such as brush and shovel (see the boy on the far left).

were sheltered from the weather). It is hard to date the print precisely. The orchestral ensemble combines two horns (back left), a standard orchestral feature in the second half of the eighteenth century, with a lute and two bass viols (in front of the horns), which were largely obsolete by then. But the inclusion of the bladder-and-string, a street instrument associated with burlesque music for much of the century (see **9, 32**), tells us that this not a band to be taken seriously. The overdressed appearance of audience and performers indicates how public concerts, whether indoors or at pleasure gardens, had become increasingly important events in the social calendar of the gentry.

35. **The Quiet Street**. 1856. Hand coloured print, John Leech (1817–64). Three of the songs being sung on the right hand side had been published earlier in the 1850s. 'Red, White and Blue' refers to the chorus of a patriotic song known in British and American versions. The British version (1852) begins 'Britannia, the pride of the ocean', and the older American version (1843, and still well-known) 'Columbia, the gem of the ocean'. The ballad 'Villikins and his Dinah' (first published 1853) had been popularized by the comic actor and singer Frederick Robson in the play *The Wandering Minstrel*, and 'Pop goes the Weasel' was originally published as an 'old English dance' (1853).

36. ***The Consort***. Date
unknown. Print, Thomas
Bakewell (*fl.* 1729–64).
Today, the title would read
'The Concert'; the words
'consort' and 'concert' were
used interchangeably in the
eighteenth century.

HE CONSORT | Each tuneful Instrument imparts | While on our Ears the Sounds improve,
The pleasing Passion to our hearts; | Soft Musick melts the mind to Love.

53

37. *Playing in Parts*. From
Caricatures of Gillray. *c*.1818.
James Gillray (1757–1815). The
title applies to the audience
as well as the performers: a
flirtatious transaction takes
place on the far left, while on
the right the gentleman's sword
has raised a woman's skirt.
The dog joins in the music, and
suggests too the line 'The little
dog laughed to see such sport'
from 'Hey diddle diddle'.

6

Mind Your Manners

The musicians we have just seen in three eighteenth-century English satirical prints **(32, 33, 36)** have been low- or middle-ranking professionals, performing out of doors. From the last years of the century onwards the spotlight frequently shifts indoors, to focus on domestic music-making by amateurs. The middle classes were burgeoning, and leading caricaturists such as James Gillray, Thomas Rowlandson, and the Cruikshanks (Isaac and his son George) all used music to send up bourgeois pretensions. In *Playing in Parts* **(37)**, Gillray caricatures the intense concentration, ungraceful physical gestures, and distorted facial expressions captured from a frozen moment of performance.

Animal imagery and mock instruments continue to play a part in humour directed at ensemble

38. ***Musical Mousers***.
?1820s. Lithograph, W. Aldous, lithographer (*fl.* 1824–7), after design by Carle Vernet (1758–1836). In later life Carle Vernet produced many satirical prints of everyday life. Earlier, he had made his name as a painter of horses and their riders. He himself was an active and vigorous horseman until his death at the age of 78.

40. ***A train-band captain eke was he***. Date unknown. Pen and wash, Thomas Rowlandson (1756–1827). The drawing belongs to a pair of illustrations for William Cowper's ballad *John Gilpin* (1782). The title of the drawing comes from the first verse:

John Gilpin was a citizen
Of credit and renown,
A train-band captain eke was he
Of famous London town.

'Train-band' was the term for a trained company of citizen soldiers, found in London from the sixteenth to eighteenth centuries. The illustration does not relate to the story that follows, which concerns John Gilpin's adventures on a runaway horse as he tries to meet up with his wife and children for a wedding anniversary celebration.

39. *Vacuum Quartet.* 1956.
Gerard Hoffnung (1925–59).
From *The Hoffnung Music
Festival*. The composer
Malcolm Arnold gave an
ethereal moment to three
vacuum cleaners and an
electric floor polisher in his
Grand Grand Overture,
commissioned to open the
first concert that Hoffnung
organized at the Royal Festival
Hall (1956). Other mock
instruments in the programme
included stone hot water
bottles, a hosepipe, a consort
of broken glass, and air-raid
sirens. The concert was hugely
successful, although some
of the pieces demonstrated
that, whereas musical humour
on the page makes its point
in an instant, the smile at the
start of a humorous musical
performance freezes into a
rictus if the joke is extended for
any length of time.

music-making during the nineteenth and twentieth
centuries. In Carle Vernet's *Musical Mousers* **(38)**,
concentration has been disrupted. Although some
of the cats play on (including the spectacled pianist,
the blissful fiddler, the trumpeter, and double bass
player), the singer has noticed a mouse, while the
mandolin player and another fiddler have dropped
their instruments to catch it. More than 100 years
later, Gerard Hoffnung updated the mock instrument
tradition with twentieth-century domestic
equipment in the form of vacuum cleaners, played by
an amateur quartet **(39)**.

Returning to the late eighteenth century and
moving outdoors again, Thomas Rowlandson
sketches 'a citizen of credit and renown', John Gilpin,
captaining an ill-assorted group of army volunteers
(40). Two plain youths on fife and drum lead the
procession; they do not take the event quite as
seriously as the self-important Gilpin. In *Music Pieces
No. 1* **(41)**, civilian and military worlds meet in an
exchange between two animated instruments, an
elegant violin and a smartly-dressed drum:

'Glad to see you look so well, Humdrum, after your beating on the Parade!'

'Thank ye Cat-gut! Bless me what a Beau/Bow you've got since we last met!'

The apparent mistake ('Beau' replaced by 'Bow') is probably deliberate, to emphasise the wordplay. The most familiar stereotype of violin-playing elegance for illustrators (an antithesis to the one-legged fiddler) had for many years been the dancing master, who taught ballroom dances from his miniature 'kit' or violin. In *The Dancing Lesson*, George Cruikshank satirized polite society through the exaggerated postures adopted by a dancing master and his young pupils as they practise an essential social accomplishment **(42)**.

41. *Music Pieces No. 1*. ?1840s. Hand-coloured print, sold by W. Spooner (*fl.* 1843–5). This is the first of four prints based on animated musical instruments. All the captions involve feeble puns.

42. ***The Dancing Lesson***, Parts 1 and 2. 1822. Hand-coloured prints, George Cruikshank (1792–1878). Dancing masters, as dance professionals, taught ballet too. By the late eighteenth century stage dancers could execute a full 180-degree turn-out of the feet; the position is demonstrated by teacher and pupils in the first print, and is forced on an unhappy girl with her feet in a trough in the second.

7
Victorian Ventures

The increasing number of children's books published
in the nineteenth century included countless nursery
rhyme collections. A few of the rhymes incorporate
animal instrumentalists, as for example

> Hey diddle diddle,
> The cat and the fiddle,
> The cow jumped over the moon;
> The little dog laughed to see such sport,
> And the dish ran away with the spoon.[7]

Theories abound about the meaning and antiquity of
the rhyme. One Victorian antiquary and folklorist,
James Orchard Halliwell, proposed that the first
line derived from ancient Greek. The Opies, in their
Oxford Dictionary of Nursery Rhymes, scorned all such
notions: 'Probably the best-known nonsense verse
in the language, a considerable amount of nonsense
has been written about it.'[8] It first appeared in
print *c.*1765, but fiddling cats go back much further.
Examples survive from the fourteenth century
as carvings on misericords in Hereford and Wells
cathedrals.

The standard of illustration in children's books
rose sharply in the second half of the nineteenth
century (compare **43** and **44**), thanks chiefly to

43. Frontispiece to Marshall's *Mother Goose's Melody*. 1816. This grotesque print conflates elements of two nonsense rhymes, 'Hey diddle diddle' and 'The sow came in with a saddle'. The latter begins;

> The sow came in with the saddle,
> The little pig rocked the cradle,
> The dish jumped up on the table,
> To see the pot swallow the ladle.

(Iona and Peter Opie, *The Oxford Dictionary of Nursery Rhymes* (Oxford, 1951), 395–6).

44. From *The Hey Diddle Diddle Picture Book*. *c.*1882. Drawn by Randolph Caldecott (1846–86), engraved and printed by Edmund Evans (1826–1905). Randolph Caldecott illustrated the story of each nursery rhyme in a series of images, and from time to time added his own satirical allusions to Victorian society. At the end of 'Hey diddle diddle', after the dish has run away the spoon, Caldecott shows the spoon's parents (father knife and mother fork) angrily reclaiming their wayward daughter. The dish lies shattered on the floor, having been dealt a mortal blow by the father.

High Diddle, Diddle, the Cat and the Fiddle.
The Cow Jumped over the Moon;
The Little Dog Laugh'd to see such Craft,
And the Dish ran away with the spoon.

the efforts of one man, the engraver and publisher Edmund Evans. In the 1860s Evans developed a method of colour printing that produced high-quality images at low cost, and with his entrepreneurial flair found three talented young illustrators to exploit his technique: Walter Crane, Kate Greenaway, and Randolph Caldecott. The latter produced the liveliest work of the trio **(44)**, and achieved an international reputation before his early death at the age of 39.

When Caldecott moved to London from Manchester near the start of his career, he met the author and *Punch* cartoonist George du Maurier, and

was influenced by the latter's acute observations of the Victorian social scene. Du Maurier often used domestic music in his satire **(45)** but his cartoons, like many of the time, mean little without their captions. His idiosyncratic capitalization of initials and use of italics – 'I want *you* to Sing next!' – reflect perfectly the emphases of the anxious hostess. Try reading the whole caption out loud.

Victorian solemnity sometimes makes it hard, from our perspective, to discern if an eccentric musical activity is being taken seriously or mocked. At first, a poster for the monstrous Rock

Music at Home. (No. 3.)

Music at Home.

No. III.

("To such base uses do we come at last.")

HOSTESS (*whispering, to Distinguished Amateur*). "I want *you* to Sing next!"

DISTINGUISHED AMATEUR (*whose Voice is not quite what it used to be*). "I thought I wasn't to Sing till quite at the end."

HOSTESS. "Yes—but there *are not Ices enough*—and I want *some of the People to go!*"

No. 95.

45. **From *English Society at Home*.** 1880. George Du Maurier (1834–96).

46. **Poster for the Rock Harmonicon**. 1840s. Joseph Richardson (c.1790–1855) developed his giant xylophone from lumps of slate found on Skiddaw, one of the highest fells in the English Lake District. He and his three sons toured Britain giving concerts on the Rock Harmonicon from 1840 to 1862. During the late 1840s further percussion effects were added and the group became the Richardson and Sons, Rock, Bell and Steel Band. The Rock Harmonicon survives in Keswick Museum and is still playable.

Harmonicon (**46**) seems faintly ludicrous, with its reference to inventor Joseph Richardson's 'Thirteen Years' incessant toil' and a programme that includes Mozart's overture to *The Magic Flute*. Yet an endorsement from composer Sir George Smart ('the production of the "Rock Harmonicon" does infinite credit to your perseverance and musical feeling') and a concert before Queen Victoria and Prince Albert at Buckingham Palace suggest that performances by Richardson and his sons were taken seriously.

8

Soulful Soloists

47. **From *Old Mother Hubbard***. 1865. Illustrations attributed to Alfred Crowquill, pseudonym for Alfred Henry Forrestier (1804–72). The nursery rhyme 'Old Mother Hubbard' was first published to great success in 1805, as by 'S. C. M.' (Sarah Catherine Martin (1768–1826), according to the Opies). The first verse remains well-known:
Old Mother Hubbard
Went to the cupboard,
To fetch her poor dog a bone;
But when she came there
The cupboard was bare
And so the poor dog had none.
The remaining 13 verses are largely forgotten. Mother Hubbard goes on errands to buy the dog all manner of items, and on each occasion

The final images focus on contrasting types of musician and music-lover in the nineteenth and twentieth centuries: the amateur, the celebrity, and the person they depend on, an enthusiastic listener. In many cheap editions of the popular nursery rhyme 'Old Mother Hubbard', the flautist dog is depicted unimaginatively, playing upright in front of a music stand. The flute was the most popular instrument with gentleman amateurs during the nineteenth century, and a better-quality illustration, attributed to the caricaturist and writer Alfred Crowquill, portrays a foppish hound playing from music resting untidily on the floor **(47)**.

Until the development of recorded sound, amateurs and professional virtuosi alike were soon forgotten after their deaths. Exceptionally though, the image of Niccolò Paganini lived on, as a prototype for the wild, long-haired genius with a flamboyant and dissipated lifestyle **(48)**. The toppled candle and broken strings in the illustration may refer to an unfortunate concert in Italy, described by Paganini himself: 'A nail had run into my shoe, and I came on limping, at which the audience laughed. At the moment I was about to commence my concerto, the candles of my desk fell out. Another laugh. After the first few bars of my solo my first string broke,

she returns to find him performing a human activity: smoking a pipe, standing on his head, feeding the cat, and playing the flute. (Opie, *Oxford Dictionary of Nursery Rhymes*, 317).

48. **Cover for song 'The Wonderful Paganini'**. 1831. Niccolò Paganini (1782–1840) made his public debut as a violinist aged 11 and undertook his first professional tour at the age of 15. He was mobbed in the streets on his first visit to London in 1831, and the chorus of this topical song runs: *What a hubbub! what a fuss! all London sure are frantic, sirs, The Prince of Fiddlers has arriv'd, great Paganini's come.* He proceeded to give 59 concerts throughout Britain and Ireland within six months, and bought several properties from the proceeds. Although this copy of *The Wonderful Paganini* was published in Boston USA, William Thomas Moncrieff (1794–1857), who wrote the lyrics, was a Londoner and author of some 200 plays.

" Well actually, Miss Tonks, my Soul is in torment."

which increased the hilarity; but I played the piece on three strings and the sneers quickly changed to general applause.'[9] At the opposite end of the fiddler spectrum is Ronald Searle's St Trinian's schoolgirl **(49)**, whose 'soul in torment' brings to mind George Bernard Shaw's comment that 'Hell is full of musical amateurs'.[10] Opera singers have had their share of insults too, particularly from composers and conductors: 'how wonderful opera would be if there were no singers' (Rossini);[11] 'you are quite right to prefer dogs' (Debussy);[12] and 'a tenor is not a man but a disease' (von Bülow).[13] In his gentle way, Gerard Hoffnung continues the insults with a tenor who adjusts expression and emotion through four waistcoat buttons that function like the control knobs of an old-fashioned record player, labelled 'off/on', 'ppp/fff', 'sobs', and 'wobble' **(50)**. Finally, an image that evokes the early era of sound reproduction, yet at the same time foretells with astonishing prescience the advent of the personal stereo **(51)**; it forms the cover illustration to an American two-step dance for piano. Thomas Edison had invented the cylinder phonograph in 1877, but in the 1890s Émil Berliner started producing flat disc gramophone records that could be mass-produced from masters. By the time of 'Uncle Silas' in 1913 the old wax cylinder had become

an outdated technology, appropriate only for an
elderly 'rube' (country bumpkin). Today, gramophone
records and even compact discs seem outmoded
beside miniaturized personal stereo and digital
music storage devices. An early twenty-first century
American cartoon shows a boy, headphones plugged
into a tiny white box, looking around his father's
roomful of vinyl records. 'Wow Dad, you have almost
as much music here as I have in my iPod'.[14]

This brief survey has shown that while themes
and topics of humorous musical imagery recur, focus
and purpose alter as the centuries progress. Musical
antics in medieval marginalia seem generally playful,
although our ignorance of the period means that
satirical allusions may not be perceived. In graphic
art of the Renaissance and baroque eras the use of
music as a weapon in moral, social, and political
satire becomes more obvious. Illustrators and artists
habitually drew on professionals at the lower end of
the social scale to aid their message, but occasionally
they dared to include the director or patron too.
Allusions to the noisy *charivari* or rough music ritual
in the form of kitchen equipment as burlesque
instruments may reinforce the ridicule. Towards the
end of the eighteenth century, amateur musicians
attract the attention of caricaturists. They enter
the frame at the very time that the word 'amateur'
itself starts to acquire pejorative overtones; it had
originally been a term of praise, applied to someone
who practised an art for love rather than money. In
the following century, as opportunities for travel
expanded, international virtuosi join the ranks of
mocked singers and instrumentalists. Yet, through
all social, cultural, and technological changes, the
neediest and least able performers persist as figures
of fun; they appear as humans, hybrids, and animals

49. **From *Souls in Torment***.
1953. Ronald Searle (b. 1920).
Searle felt pigeonholed by the
success of the girls' school St
Trinian's, and in the cartoon
collection *Souls in Torment* a
nuclear bomb destroys the
school. But its life was far
from over: five films appeared
between 1954 and 1980,
starting with *The Belles of St
Trinian's* (1954), which starred
Alastair Sim and Joyce Grenfell.

50. **From *The Hoffnung
Music Festival***. 1956. Gerard
Hoffnung (1925–59). *The
Hoffnung Music Festival* was
the third of six small books of
musical cartoons that Gerard
Hoffnung had published
between 1953 and 1959. The
tenor heads the 'Bel Canto'
section.

in about half the illustrations selected for this book.

The rustic Uncle Silas himself recalls Shakespeare's 'rude mechanical' Bottom with his 'rural music' in *A Midsummer Night's Dream*. Musical humour is no joke for some.

Notes

1 William Shakespeare, *A Midsummer Night's Dream*, Act 4, Scene 1. Charlie Hinman (ed.), *The Norton Facsimile:The First Folio of Shakespeare* (London, 1968), 157 (spellings modernized).

2 Michael Camille, *Image on the Edge* (London, 1992), 12.

3 In, for example, Camille, *Image on the Edge*, 61–2, and Alixe Bovey, *Monsters and Grotesques in Medieval Manuscripts* (London, 2002), 42.

4 Allardyce Nicoll, *Masks, Mimes and Miracles* (London, 1931), 165.

5 Quoted in David Bindman (ed.), *Encyclopaedia of British Art* (London, 1985), in entry on Francis Barlow.

6 From the title-page of *The Jovial Companions.* Bodleian, Harding Mus. E 91.

7 Iona and Peter Opie, *The Oxford Dictionary of Nursery Rhymes* (Oxford, 1951), 203.

8 Opie, *Dictionary of Nursery Rhymes*, 203.

9 Sir George Grove (ed.), *A Dictionary of Music and Musicians*, 4 vols (London, 1879–89), ii. Entry on Paganini.

10 Derek Watson, *Dictionary of Musical Quotations* (Edinburgh, 1991), 238.

11 Watson, *Dictionary of Musical Quotations*, 326.

12 Watson, *Dictionary of Musical Quotations*, 327.

13 Ned Shapiro, *An Encyclopaedia of Quotations about Music* (Newton Abbot, 1978), 162.

14 Nitrozac and Snaggy, *The Best of the Joy of Tech* (California, 2003) (no page numbers).

51. **Cover for piano piece 'Uncle Silas (Some Rube)'**. 1913. W. J. Dittmar (dates unknown). Abe Losch was one of many pseudonyms used by the composer Harry J. Lincoln (1878–1937). Lincoln also sold his compositions to others, who then put their own names to the pieces. He eventually bought out the Vandersloot company in 1929 or 1930. The illustrator W. J. Dittmar drew a number of covers for Vandersloot in the years either side of 1910.

Works Consulted

Jeremy Barlow, *The Enraged Musician: Hogarth's Musical Imagery* (Aldershot, 2005).

David Bindman (ed.), *Encyclopaedia of British Art* (London, 1985).

Alixe Bovey, *Monsters and Grotesques in Medieval Manuscripts* (London, 2002).

D. B. Brown, *Ashmolean Museum Oxford: Catalogue of the Collection of Drawings*, iv: *The Earlier British Drawings* (Oxford, 1982).

Michael Camille, *Image on the Edge* (London, 1992).

James J. Fuld, *The Book of World-Famous Music*, revised edition (New York, 1971).

Sir George Grove (ed.), *A Dictionary of Music and Musicians* (4 vols) (London, 1879–89).

Annetta Hoffnung, *Gerard Hoffnung* (London, 1998).

Howard Jacobson, *Seriously Funny* (London, 1997).

M. R. James, *The Romance of Alexander: A Collotype Facsimile of MS. Bodley 264* (Oxford, 1933).

Malcolm Jones, *The Secret Middle Ages* (Stroud, 2002).

Roy Judge, *The Jack-in-the-Green* (London, 1979).

Allardyce Nicoll, *Masks, Mimes and Miracles* (London, 1931).

Nitrozac and Snaggy (Liza Schmalcel and Bruce Evans), *The Best of the Joy of Tech* (Sebastopol (California), 2003).

Iona and Peter Opie, *The Oxford Dictionary of Nursery Rhymes* (Oxford, 1951).

Otto Pächt and J. J. G. Alexander, *Illuminated Manuscripts in the Bodleian Library Oxford*, i: *German, Dutch, Flemish, French, and Spanish Schools* (Oxford, 1966).

Otto Pächt and J. J. G. Alexander, *Illuminated Manuscripts in the Bodleian Library Oxford*, iii:, *British, Irish, and Icelandic Schools* (Oxford, 1973).

K. T. Parker, *Catalogue of the Collection of Drawings in the Ashmolean Museum*, i: *Netherlandish, German, French, and Spanish Schools* (Oxford, 1938).

K. T. Parker, *Catalogue of the Collection of Drawings in the Ashmolean Museum*, ii: *Italian Schools* (Oxford, 1956).

Tom Phillips, *Music in Art* (Munich and New York, 1997).

Ned Shapiro, *An Encyclopaedia of Quotations about Music* (Newton Abbot, 1978).

Karl Storck, *Musik und Musiker in Karikatur und Satir* (Oldenburg, 1910).

Derek Watson, *Dictionary of Musical Quotations* (Edinburgh, 1991).

List of Illustrations and Sources

The locations of prints and drawings in the
Ashmolean Museum are identified by reference to
numbering in the catalogues by D. B. Brown or K. T.
Parker (see Works Consulted), unless they are from
uncatalogued material in the Douce Collection, in
which case the Douce Box references are given.

1. Fox blows horn (p. 13). Bodleian, MS. Ashm. 1525,
   fol. 12r.
2. Fiddler, imitated by ape with stick (p. 14).
   Bodleian, MS. Douce 6, fol. 76r.
3. Mock fiddler with bellows and tongs (p. 15).
   Bodleian, MS. Douce 366, fol. 9v.
4. *Scraps and Sketches Part 3* (p. 16). Ashmolean, Douce
   Box W.1.2 (Box 1), 162.
5. Hybrid fiddler (p. 17). Bodleian, MS. Douce 77,
   fol. 49r.
6. Demon plays hand-bells at angel trumpeter (p. 18).
   Bodleian, MS. Douce 5, fol. 100v.
7. Gittern player accompanies dancers (p. 20).
   Bodleian, MS. Bodl. 264, fol. 21v.
8. Musicians frame dice players (p. 20). Bodleian,
   MS. Bodl. 264, fol. 109v.
9. *The Beggar's Opera* burlesqued (p. 21). British
   Museum (the copy in the Ashmolean, Hogarth
   Box, was not available for reproduction at the
   time of publication).
10. Pipe and taborer accompanies dancing bear
    (p.22). Bodleian, MS. Bodl. 264, fol. 117v.
11. *The Bear and his Leader* (p. 23). From *Caricatures of
    Gillray,* p. 111. Bodleian, John Johnson Collection.
12. Performing sow with suckling piglets (p. 24).
    Bodleian, MS. Bodl. 264, fol. 124v.
13. Cover illustration for *Three Little Pigs Went to*

30. A political satire (pp. 42 – 3). Ashmolean, Brown 63.
31. Antimasque scene (p. 45). William Davenant, *Britannia Triumphans* (London, 1638). Bodleian, Douce I 227 pp. 10–11.
32. Frontispiece for *The Jovial Companions or Merry Club* (p. 46). Bodleian, Harding Mus. E 91.
33. *Industry & Idleness 6: The Industrious 'Prentice out of his Time and Married to his Master's Daughter* (pp. 48–9). Ashmolean, Hogarth Box.
34. *May-Day in London* (p. 50). Ashmolean, Douce Box E.1.1, 49.
35. *The Quiet Street* (p. 51). Bodleian, John Johnson Collection, Trades and Professions Box 6 (69).
36. *The Consort* (pp. 52–3). Ashmolean, Douce Box E.1.4, 293.
37. *Playing in Parts* (p. 54). From *Caricatures of Gillray*, p. 55. Bodleian, John Johnson Collection.
38. *Musical Mousers* (p. 55). Bodleian, John Johnson Collection, Musical Instruments Box 2.
39. *Vacuum Quartet* (p. 58). Gerard Hoffnung, *The Hoffnung Music Festival* (London 1956), pp. 44–5. Bodleian, 17075 f.17.
40. *A train-band captain eke was he* (pp. 56–7). Ashmolean, Rowlandson Box (35), Brown 1575 (titled 'A Captain Train Band eke was he' in Brown).
41. *Music Pieces No. 1* (p. 59). Bodleian, John Johnson Collection, in Puzzle Pictures Box.
42. *The Dancing Lesson*, Parts 1 and 2 (p. 60). Bodleian, John Johnson Collection, Dancing Box.
43. Frontispiece to Marshall's *Mother Goose's Melody* (p. 62). Bodleian, Opie Collection, N898 (microfiche 020 009).
44. From *The Hey Diddle Diddle Picture Book* (p. 63). Randolph Caldecott. Bodleian, Opie Collection, N77 (microfiche 018 257–9).

45. 'To such base uses do we come at last' (p. 64). George du Maurier *English Society at Home* (London, 1880), p. 37. Bodleian, Arts.d.133.

46. Poster for the Rock Harmonicon (p. 65). Bodleian, John Johnson Collection, Musical Instruments Box 2.

47. Dog flautist (p. 66), from *Old Mother Hubbard*, 3rd opening. Bodleian, Opie Collection, N357 (microfiche 019 027).

48. Cover illustration for 'The Wonderful Paganini' (p. 67). Bodleian, Harding American songs Collection, Comic Vocal Box (83).

49. 'Well actually, Miss Tonks, my soul is in torment' (p. 68). Ronald Searle, *Souls in Torment* (London, 1953), p. 95. Bodleian, 17075 d.246.

50. Operatic tenor (p. 69). Gerard Hoffnung, *The Hoffnung Music Festival* (London 1956), p. 21. Bodleian, 17075 f.17.

51. Cover illustration for 'Uncle Silas (Some Rube)' (p. 70). Bodleian, Harding American songs Collection, Phonograph Box (222).

Glossary of Obsolete Instruments
(Figures refer to illustration numbers)

Bagpipe (9, 13, 17, 22, 23). Present in many parts of Europe during the Middle Ages and Renaissance. In Britain, the bagpipe disappeared northwards during the eighteenth century, but survived in Northumberland and Scotland.

Bladder-and-string (9, 32, 36). Consists of a string fastened to both ends of a long stick, with an inflated pig's bladder inserted between string and stick towards one end; played with a bow. Often used as self-accompaniment to singing.

Bombard (17). The largest member of the shawm family (see below).

Bones (26). Clappers made from animal ribs, similar in operation to castanets.

Cittern. Small, wire-strung instrument, plucked with a plectrum and associated with popular music in the Renaissance. Although it is not now thought to be a descendant of the gittern (see below), it often had, like the latter, a grotesque carved head on the peg box.

Dulcimer (9). An instrument with wire strings stretched over bridges on a trapezoid-shaped sound box. The strings are hit with light, hand-held hammers. Large versions survive as the cimbalom in eastern Europe today. See 'psaltery' below.

Fiddle (medieval) (2, 5). Bowed, gut-strung instrument, with a body that may or may not have a waisted, guitar-like shape.

Gittern. (7, 8). A small, gut-strung instrument of the Middle Ages, plucked with a plectrum.

Hurdy-gurdy (24, 25). A wheel, turned with a handle, rubs against a number of strings. Tunes are played by depressing keys that bring tangents into contact with the highest string. Other strings bypass the tangents and produce the same note or drone continuously.

Jew's harp (9, 26). Of ancient origin, and found universally; it is neither Jewish nor a harp. Sound is produced from a vibrating metal strip (lamella) which is held in a small frame. The instrument is placed in the opening of the mouth and the lamella is plucked with the finger. The mouth acts as a resonator or amplifier.

Kit (42). A miniature violin, used by dancing masters. The instrument was small enough to be kept in a tailcoat pocket.

Lute (27, 36). Gut-strung and plucked with the fingers, the lute was ubiquitous in secular Renaissance music-making. It gradually became obsolete during the eighteenth century. The instrument shown in 27 is either an archlute or small theorbo (see below); it has additional bass or 'diapason' strings that stretch out to a second peg box. These strings bypass the fingerboard, so cannot be stopped with the left hand.

Marrowbone and cleaver (33). Played by apprentice butchers' boys in the eighteenth century, for celebration or protest. On some occasions the cleavers were tuned to play particular notes.

Pipe and tabor (10, 20, 31). The three-holed pipe, blown like a recorder and self-accompanied with a tabor (drum), is often shown accompanying rustic dance in iconography from the thirteenth to nineteenth centuries. Some instruments in medieval illustrations are better interpreted as ancestors of the Catalan flaviol, which is shorter, thicker, and has more holes.

Positive organ (15). The mid-sized instrument of the Middle Ages and Renaissance, larger than the miniature portative organ, but smaller than the principal organ in a church or cathedral.

Psaltery (8). Similar in construction, materials, and sometimes shape, to the dulcimer (see above). The chief difference is that the strings are plucked (with fingers or plectrum), not hit. The psaltery and dulcimer belong to the zither family.

Rebec (16). Bowed, gut-strung instrument, with a pear-shaped body. The rebec probably developed from the Arab *rabāb* in the thirteenth century. It survived into the baroque era as a street instrument.

Rock Harmonicon (46). For a fuller description of this giant xylophone, see the caption to the illustration on p. 65.

Saltbox (9, 18, 32). The wooden kitchen saltbox with a hinged lid was used for musical burlesque and for publicizing street theatre in England during the eighteenth and early nineteenth centuries. A wooden spoon provided the beater.

Shawm (1, 17, 29, 32). A raucous double-reed wind instrument, ancestor of the oboe. It was played in medieval, Renaissance, and early Baroque music at outdoor performances, or at banquets, balls, and other festive occasions held in large interior spaces.

Theorbo. Similar in appearance to the archlute (see 'lute' above). It may not be easy to distinguish the two iconographically, though the theorbo usually had a larger body. The top two courses of strings are tuned an octave lower than on the lute or archlute.

Viol (31, 36). A family of bowed, gut-strung instruments popular in the Renaissance and early Baroque periods; the largest survives as the double bass. Though superficially similar in appearance to the violin family, viols usually had six strings, fretted fingerboards, and were played on the lap or between the legs (hence the Italian name *viola da gamba*).

Index

For musical instruments, mock instruments, and noise–producing devices, see under 'instruments and performers'. For individual animals, see under 'animals'. Italicized figures refer to page numbers for illustrations and captions.